X

A World of Difference

Welcome Home!

By Sylvia White

CHILDRENS PRESS®
CHICAGO

Picture Acknowledgements

Cover (top), NASA; Cover (top right), © Robert Frerck/Odyssey/Frerck/Chicago; Cover (bottom left), © Bruce Leighty/MGA/Photri; Cover (bottom right), © Christine Osborne/Valan; 1, © Robert Frerck/Odyssey/Frerck/Chicago; 3 (top), Wendy Stone/Odyssey/Chicago; 3 (bottom left), © Robert Frerck/Odyssey/Frerck/Chicago; 3 (bottom right), © Wendy Stone/Odyssey/Chicago; 4 (left), © Kevin R. Downey Photography; 4 (right), © Cameramann International, Ltd., 5 (top), Steve Vidler/SuperStock International, Inc.; 6 (top), © Alan Levenson/Tony Stone Images; 6 (bottom left), Kurt Scholz/SuperStock International, Inc.; 6 (bottom right), The Bettmann Archive; 7 (top), © Jason Laure'/Laure' Communications; 7 (bottom), © Wendy Stone/Odyssey/Chicago; 8 (left), © Ann Purcell; 8 (right), © Charles Preitner/Visuals Unlimited; 9 (top), © Steve McCutcheon/Visuals Unlimited; 9 (center), © N. Pecnik/Visuals Unlimited; 9 (bottom), Steve Vidler/SuperStock International, Inc.; 10 (top), © Virginia R. Grimes; 10 (bottom), © David Hanson/Tony Stone Images; 11 (top and bottom), © Jason Laure'/Laure' Communications; 12 (left and right), © Cameramann International, Ltd.; 13 (left), © Bob & Ira Spring; 13 (right), © Donna Carroll/Travel Stock; 14 (left), © Steve Bourgeois/Unicorn Stock Photos; 14 (right), © Wendy Stone/Odyssey/Chicago; 15 (top), © Laurence Hughs/SuperStock International, Inc.; 15 (center), © C. Osborne/Valan; 15 (bottom) and 16 (left), © Robert Frerck/Frerck/Chicago; 16 (right), © Carl Purcell; 17 (top), © J. Eastcott/Y. Momatiuk/Valan; 17 (center), © Greg Meadors/PhotoEdit; 17 (bottom), © Joyce Photographics/Valan; 18 (top), World Photo Services LTD/SuperStock International, Inc.; 18 (bottom), © Jeff Greenberg/PhotoEdit; 19 (top right), © Deborah L. Martin/Unicorn Stock Photos; 19 (bottom), © Mary & Lloyd McCarthy/Root Resources; 20 (left), © Kevin R. Downey Photography; 20 (right), © Deborah L. Martin/Unicorn Stock Photos; 21 (top), © Phillip Norton/Valan; 21 (bottom left), © Kurt Scholz/SuperStock International, Inc.; 21 (bottom right), Reuters/Bettmann; 22 (top left), © Brian Atkinson/Valan; 22 (top right), © Byron Crader/Root Resources; 22 (bottom left), © Robert Frerck/Odyssey/Frerck/Chicago; 22 (bottom right), © James P. Rowan/MGA/Photri; 23 (left and right), © Robert Frerck/Odyssey/Frerck/Chicago; 24 (top), © Christine Osborne/Valan; 24 (bottom), © Steve Vidler/SuperStock International, Inc.; 25 (left), © Tony Freeman/PhotoEdit; 25 (right), SuperStock International, Inc.; 26 (top), © Porterfield/Chickering; 26 (bottom left), © Mary & Lloyd McCarthy/Root Resources; 26 (bottom right), © Alain Le Garsmeur/Tony Stone Images; 27 (top), © Byron Crader/Root Resource; 27 (center), Photri; 27 (bottom) © Porterfield/Chickering; 28 (top), © D & I Mac Donald/Photri; 28 (bottom), © Carl Purcell; 29 (right), © Robert Frerck/Odyssey/Frerck/Chicago; 30 (top), © David Young-Wolff/PhotoEdit; 30 (bottom), © Buddy Mays/Travel Stock; 31 (top right), © LINK/Visuals Unlimited; 31 (bottom), © Cameramann International, Ltd.

On the cover

Top: Village house, Yucatan, Mexico
Bottom left: High-rise apartment building,
    Singapore
Bottom right: Venda chief's house, Zimbabwe

On the title page

 Village house, Yucatan, Mexico

Project Editor Shari Joffe
Design Herman Adler Design Group
Photo Research Feldman & Associates

White, Sylvia.
    Welcome home! / by Sylvia White.
        p. cm. — (A world of difference)
    Includes index.
    ISBN 0-516-08193-4
       1. Dwellings — Juvenile literature.   [1. Dwellings.]
  I. Title. II. Series.
GT172.W48 1995
391.36 — dc20   94-38290
                                                                            CIP
                                                                             AC

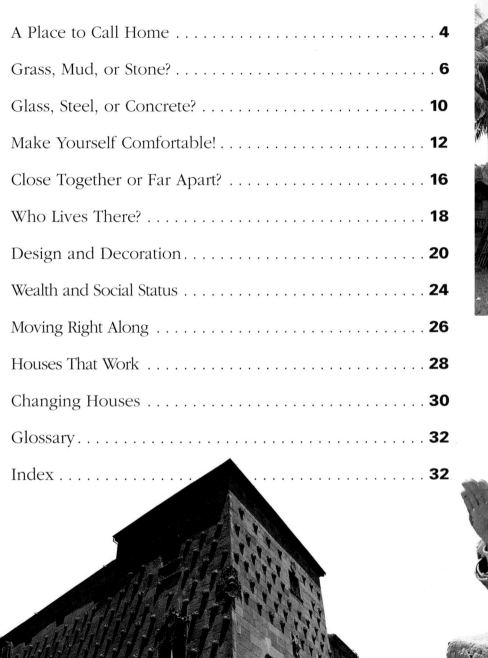

A Place to Call Home

If you could have any kind of home you wanted, what would it be like? Would you build it yourself or would you ask an architect or builder to build it for you? Would you use brick, or stone, or grass and logs? Would it be tall or small? Where would you make doors and windows? Would you rather move into a home that is already built?

These are questions everyone who wants a home asks, for a home must suit the daily lives of the people who live in it. For example, if you live in a hot, wet climate, you build a home to protect you from the sun and rain. In a cold climate, your home needs to protect you from the snow and wind. A home is where you eat and sleep. It keeps you safe and gives you a place to store your possessions. A home can be a place to entertain your friends and a way of displaying your taste or your social status. It might even be the place where you work!

Prehistoric cave dwelling, Spain (below left) Natural caves have been used for shelter ever since humans began populating the earth thousands of years ago. Even in prehistoric times, people made changes to the entrances and the insides of the caves to make their lives more comfortable. This cave, near Santander, Spain, was lived in as early as 35,000 years ago!

Volcanic tufa dwellings, Cappadocia, Turkey Nearly 2,000 years ago, monks in this part of Turkey began carving houses out of soft volcanic rock. Some people continue to live in the ancient houses today, while others carve out new houses in the same style. The doors are placed up high for protection. People enter by ladder or stairs.

Modern apartment building, Canada Many people all over the world live in houses or apartments constructed by professional builders. Concrete, brick, lumber, stone, metal, and glass are the most common materials used in these homes.

Throughout the world, people build homes of different sizes and shapes. There are big homes so that all the grandmas, grandpas, sisters, uncles, and cousins can live together under one roof. There are small homes where just one or two people live. There are long homes, tall homes, square homes, and even round homes. People use all kinds of building materials too, depending on what is available where they live. Some people use bricks, others use bamboo sticks, and some use hides from animals. A home, then, can tell us something about where and how people live. Let's look at ways people around the world have built their homes to fit their lives.

Grass, Mud, or Stone?

Often, people build their homes from whatever natural materials they find nearby, like plants, stones, animal hides or even the soil itself. The fact that different natural materials are found in different environments is one reason why people's homes vary from place to place.

In tropical regions, which are hot and rainy, grasses, reeds, vines, and tall trees grow abundantly, and the soil is often a red clay. A house builder in this type of environment commonly uses strong reeds or grasses, like bamboo, to build a lattice structure. The red clay is used to fill in spaces in the lattice, or is formed into thick bricks for walls. Vines and grasses are used to weave floor mats, and a thatched roof is made from bundled grasses and reeds.

In hot, dry, deserts, the types of plants and animals used for building material are very limited, though there are usually grasses, small trees, and lots of sand and rock. Desert people might use the fur or hair of their animals to weave cloth for tents. When they can find water, they mix the earth with it to form bricks to build cool houses with thick walls.

Bamboo house, Thailand This house has a teakwood framework, bamboo walls, and a roof thatched with straw. Trees and grasses grow abundantly and are common building materials in hot, wet countries like Thailand.

Totora reed house, Peru The Uru people live along Lake Titicaca. They build their homes out of dried totora, a type of reed that grows in dense bunches along the lake.

Masai house The Masai people of Kenya and Tanzania live mainly by herding cattle. They depend on their herds not only for food, but also for shelter—their homes are made of branches plastered over with cattle dung. The dung dries to a hard, waterproof covering that helps keep away termites.

Building a mud-brick house, Bolivia High in the Andes mountains of South America, the Quechua people build thick-walled houses out of mud-and-straw bricks.

19th-century "sodbusters," United States On the Nebraska prairie, where there were few trees, many American settlers cut sod into blocks and used the blocks to build their homes. These pioneers were nicknamed "sodbusters."

Different materials exist in cold climates. In the Alaskan and Siberian tundra, for example, there are few trees and only short grasses. Traditionally, people there have built their homes from a combination of earth and walrus skins or moose hides. Sometimes they use the most abundant material—ice—to make their houses. Building materials are in such short supply in the tundra that people may have to transport lumber or manufactured trailers from distant places.

It can be very cold in the high mountains of Tibet, too, but there, rocks and tall trees are often available for building material. Rocks are used to build walls and sometimes slate rocks are chipped into flat shapes and used for roof tiles. Large trees can be used whole, as thick logs, or they can be sawed into boards for walls and floors.

Log house, Norway In rural Norway, where trees are plentiful, houses are often built solidly of logs. The cracks between the logs are carefully filled to keep out any cold drafts. If the house has two floors, the main living area is on the larger second floor, which is built to stay warm and above the winter snow. The first floor is used for storage.

Stone house, Ireland
Traditionally, houses in rural Ireland were built of local stone and had thatched roofs of straw. Nowadays, most Irish houses are built of brick or cement.

Inuit walrus-skin dwelling
(above) The Inuit people live in the Arctic, where building materials are scarce. Traditionally, they lived in earth huts covered with sealskin or walrus skin. Today, most Inuit live in houses made of lumber lined with fiberglass.

Inuit igloo (below) When the Inuit are hunting away from their villages, they build round shelters of ice blocks to protect them from the cold. Some igloos are made of waterproof fabric—but they are still round in shape!

In temperate regions—where it may be hot or cold depending on the season—trees, stone, clay, grasses, and even bamboo may be available. People use whatever combinations of materials are plentiful. For example, in parts of England and Ireland, people use tall-growing march reeds as thatch for roofs, and build their houses of stone. In some parts of China, houses have bamboo frames filled with clay.

Pit dwelling, Tunisia In this desert area, people have solved the problem of scarce building materials by carving homes into the earth itself. These underground homes provide shelter from sandstorms and the scorching heat of the desert.

Glass, Steel, or Concrete?

Of course, houses aren't always made from natural materials. It's also common to find homes throughout the world made from manufactured materials, like glass, steel, lumber, plastic, and cement. In fact, the very same countries that have houses built of mud and bamboo—like Thailand or China—may also have houses of concrete, glass, and aluminum. Often, these houses have electric lights and indoor plumbing with sinks, baths, and toilets.

Professional builders raising a wall, United States

Apartment building, The Netherlands This building in Rotterdam includes such manufactured materials as brick, lumber, concrete, metal, and glass.

Houses in Kenya Within the same country, you may find some houses built out of natural materials native to the environment (left), and others built out of manufactured materials (below).

Sometimes they even have air conditioning for hot weather or heat for the cold. Houses of mostly manufactured materials are usually built for people who pay others to design and construct them. Architects are the people who design houses, and builders or construction companies are the ones who build them.

There are many people who build houses by themselves or with friends using combinations of natural and manufactured materials. They may buy new materials, or they may simply find used lumber, pipes, iron, cardboard, and tires discarded by the road or in dumps. In Mexico, for example, there are houses that combine mud brick, corrugated iron, cardboard, and used tires. As months and years go by, people may add plaster to the walls, glass windows, corrugated iron roofs, ceramic tiles, and paint to make their houses comfortable and beautiful.

Make Yourself Comfortable!

As people select building materials, they also decide how the roof, walls, windows, and floors might be shaped to solve the problems presented by the climate.

In hot, damp climates, walls and floors are often constructed so that breezes can blow through. For example, in parts of Panama, floors are made of bamboo slats that allow cool air to circulate through the floor. During the day, children can play in the shade of the house.

In very cold climates, walls and floors need to be well insulated. In Poland and the Ukraine, houses have thick walls of wood or stone. Houses in cold climates

Timber house, Poland The thick wooden walls of this house are built to withstand the severe cold and heavy snows of winters in Poland.

What a cool house! In Samoa, which is hot and humid, many houses have walls made of mats. These can be rolled up and fastened to the roof beams to let the breeze blow through and keep the occupants cool!

may have underground basements that serve as a strong foundation on which the house stands. The basement also lifts the first floor above the cold ground. In Canada, the basement is a cool place to store apples, potatoes, and other foods.

Stilt house, Indonesia In many tropical areas, people live in houses built on stilts. Stilts allow cooling breezes to blow under and around the house, and protect it from flooding, snakes, and insects. If the house is built over water, the space underneath might be used to store boats. If it is on land, the people might use the space to house animals, or to store bicycles, carts, cars, or trucks.

Whitewashed houses, Greece
In hot, sunny Greece, many houses are whitewashed or painted very light colors. Light colors reflect the sun's rays so walls do not absorb their heat.

Windows vary in size and shape depending on whether the climate is hot or cold, and on the amount of light, heat, and air people want let into the house. In climates where it is extremely cold, like the southern tip of Chile, small windows keep out the cold. If it is hot, like the desert of Saudi Arabia, small windows keep out the heat and harsh light. In moist tropical places like Sri Lanka, large windows allow cooling breezes to circulate, making rooms light and airy.

Roof shapes also vary with the climate. In snowy places like Norway, Sweden, and Switzerland, roofs are steeply pitched to shed heavy snow. In rainy places like Papua New Guinea, they are sloped so that heavy rains can run off. In the sunny, hot climates of Syria and southern Italy, roofs are round so as to expose only a small portion to the sun. In the dry desert areas of Morocco, Algeria, India, and the southwestern United States, some people build flat roofs of thick clay and timber to keep rooms cool. The flat roof is also a place to dry and store corn, nuts, or vegetables.

Swiss mountain chalet In the mountainous country of Switzerland, farm houses called chalets stand alone on high mountain slopes. They have steep roofs so heavy snow and ice can slide off, and broad overhangs to keep snow from piling too close to the house.

Papua New Guinea house In places where rainfall is heavy, such as Papua New Guinea, many houses have steeply pitched roofs so that the water can run off.

Zulu *indlu*, South Africa
The Zulu people of South Africa build expertly thatched houses called *indlu*. Their domed shape helps them withstand strong winds.

Some houses in the Southern United States have roofs over a large porches or verandas where people may eat their meals or simply sit and talk protected from the sun or rain.

Beehive-shaped houses, Syria
In hot, sunny Syria, some people have shaped the roofs of their houses into cones, giving them the appearance of a beehive. This shape exposes as little surface as possible to the sun. Mud houses in hot, dry places are often round, because the walls are less likely to crack if there are no corners.

Desert village, India Homes with thick clay walls and only a few tiny windows provide insulation against the extreme heat of the desert. Flat roofs provide a cool place for sleeping at night.

Close Together or Far Apart?

Population density—the number of people who live in a given area—also affects the way houses are designed in different places. Where there is plenty of land and few people, a house might stand alone, surrounded by a farm or a forest. But in places where lots of people live within a small area—such as many of the world's cities—houses are often joined together vertically or horizontally to save space.

The idea of building houses vertically, or upward, came from the Romans centuries ago. So many people wanted to live near or in Rome that there was no room for all them to live in spacious houses. So the Romans invented the first "apartment buildings." Because these were made of earthen bricks, they were not very strong

High-rise housing, Singapore
Many people are able to live in the small country of Singapore because there are so many tall apartment buildings.

New Zealand ranch house
Though it is relatively small country, New Zealand is not densely populated. Houses are often very far away from each other.

Suburban houses, Newfoundland
Many countries have both spacious rural areas and highly populated cities. Often, the cities are surrounded by suburban areas. These tend to be less densely populated than cities, but more densely populated than rural areas. Suburbs typically have detached houses that are built close together.

Low-rise apartments, Lyon, France Apartment living in France and in other parts of Europe became common in the 1500s because cities were surrounded with walls for protection. People did not want to live outside the walls, so if the population of a city grew, the buildings had to grow upward! Now France has many cities with modern low-rise and high-rise apartment buildings.

and they could only be built two or three stories high. Today, strong materials like iron, steel, and concrete are used to build apartment houses many stories high. Lots of people live in one high-rise building, but each apartment has its own set of rooms with a separate entry into a hallway.

Row houses, London, England
England is a small country. It solved the space problem in its cities by building neighborhoods of row houses. Row houses, also called town houses, are joined together horizontally. Even though these houses share a common wall, each house has its own separate entry and living space for its occupants.

Who Lives There?

Housing design also varies throughout the world because different cultures have different ideas about who makes up a household; who lives together and how.

Who lives in your house? If you live with just your parents and siblings, you are part of a small family household. But what if all your relatives lived with you; your aunts, uncles, cousins, and grandparents? That would be an extended family household.

In the United States, Europe, and Japan, most households are small family units. Houses tend to be modest in size and include the kind of rooms people use for eating, sleeping, bathing, relaxing, and entertaining friends. In Japan, where space is limited, people use movable walls, or *shoji* screens, inside to make the kinds of rooms they need in their small houses. If a family needs a large room for entertaining, the screens are opened. If a small bedroom for children is needed, the screens are closed or moved to create a small space.

In some cultures, houses are built especially for large family groups. The young, old, all the relatives, and even some close friends live together. As you can imagine, that means everyone must try to cooperate. For example, in Nigeria, some houses are built around a central courtyard. Each room around the courtyard

Small family household, Lithuania

Inside a traditional Japanese house You can see how the screens form movable walls to close off space or to open it to make large rooms. This makes a Japanese house very flexible, and also allows people to make use of all the limited space.

Iban longhouse, Malaysia The Iban people of Malaysia live in huge longhouses. Between 20 and 50 small families live in one longhouse. There are separate rooms for each family along the walls, and an open, communal space— like a street—down the center.

Living compound, Burkina Faso The compound, a common type of housing in west African countries, is a group of rooms linked by walls. Each room around this compound belongs to a different wife of the head of the compound. Small children live with their mother. When a son marries, he creates another room for himself and his wife. Each compound in a village may house an extended family of 15 to 20 people.

belongs to a member of the family. The extended family members cooperate to prepare food and see that the children of the household play safely in the courtyard.

Design and Decoration

Just as the number and relationship of the people in a household affects the design of a house, so do cultural preferences and religious beliefs. For example, in China, the ancient practice of *feng shui* may determine the direction the house should face, the location of the doors, the location of interior halls and rooms, and even the design of the garden.

Houses in Laos usually have inside at least one sacred place or shrine dedicated to an important religious figure. Flowers, fruit, and sweet-smelling incense are placed before the figure daily. In Ivory Coast, some households build small, round shapes of mud that contain the bones of their ancestors outside the entry to their compounds. Food, drink, and chicken blood are left on the shrine to ensure the ancestor's favorable help.

Religious shrine in a Japanese home In Japan, a home may have a small shrine for private daily worship.

Traditional Chinese house *Feng shui* is an ancient set of rules for positioning houses in harmony with the universe and the currents that flow through the earth. This house was built facing south. The doors and windows are located so that good currents carrying luck, health, and wealth stay inside the house.

Decorations inside and outside of houses also may tell something about people's beliefs. A crocodile carved on the outside of a house in northern Ghana indicates the belief that this household belongs to a group of people who came from a place of crocodiles. Houses in Guatemala often have a cross above the entry door to ensure that Jesus Christ will protect the household. In Austria, barns and houses are sometimes marked with complicated star-shaped designs called hex signs. These have an ancient history as magic symbols to ward off evil.

Pennsylvania Dutch house, United States These star-shaped hex signs, which originated in Austria, are meant to guard the house against evil.

Wall decoration, India For centuries, women in Bihar, India, have decorated the walls of their homes in rural India with themes from Hindu mythology.

Carved roof poles, Indonesia The intricately carved and painted roof supports of these houses symbolize ceremonial and ancestral spirits.

Doorway of a Dogon house The Dogon people, who live in the African country of Mali, believe that each house in a Dogon village is filled with spiritual power. They carve figures on the doors and locks of their homes to honor the spirits of the their ancestors.

Ndebele house, South Africa The houses of the Ndebele people are famous for their beautiful exteriors. The women who live in these houses spend hours painting them in colorful designs.

"Cockle-shell" house, Spain Throughout history, different regions or countries have developed their own traditional styles of house decoration. This happens when a style becomes popular in a certain area and is copied over and over.

Tudor-style house, England This famous English style first became popular in the 1500s, when England was ruled by the Tudor family.

House with carved exterior, Nigeria Often, people use decorative styles to carry on cultural traditions that have been passed down from generation to generation.

Not every kind of decoration has meaning. Sometimes a style of decoration is handed down for generations among household members. In South Africa, women use their artistic imaginations to decorate their houses with colorful geometric designs that may include representations of animals or people.

House in Chiapas, Mexico Sometimes, people like to use their homes to express their own personality and artistic taste!

Wealth and Social Status

People's homes often reflect their social status— their position within their society. Some people use their home as a symbol of their wealth and power. That's why, in many cultures, the biggest or most elaborately decorated houses belong to the richest or most powerful people. Wealthy people can afford to pay architects and construction companies to design and build large houses for them. The houses may have new and expensive materials that show everyone the owner is rich. They may also have extra comforts, such as the newest kitchen equipment, expensive air conditioning, or a swimming pool. Even in cultures where people build their own homes, the homes of community leaders or other important people are often

Home of a Venda chief, Zimbabwe In many cultures, the homes of community leaders are distinguished from others by being larger or more elaborately decorated.

Blenheim Palace, England Throughout history, people have liked to show their wealth or power by building huge, expensive homes. This palace was the birthplace of Winston Churchill, Britain's prime minister in the early 1900s.

distinguished from everybody else's by being larger or having more decoration.

People of less means usually live in smaller or simpler homes. Sometimes, even very large families live in small houses. They might like to have more room, but they don't have enough money to build, buy, or rent a bigger house.

In the countries of Latin America, and in other nations too, people come to cities from rural areas hoping to find a better life. Because they are poor, they often live in small, overcrowded houses made of scraps of tin, cardboard, and wood. When many people do not work, whole towns of poor people living like this can spring up. "Shantytown" or "slum" are two of many words used to describe these settlements.

Homeless family, United States
Some people are so poor that they cannot afford any home at all. These are homeless people who, if they are lucky, may live in a car. If they are not lucky they may sleep on a piece of cardboard under a bridge. Homelessness is a serious problem in many countries throughout the world.

Shantytown, Tijuana, Mexico
The people who built these houses have used bits and pieces of found materials—like scraps of metal, lumber, and cardboard—because they can't afford to buy new building materials.

Moving Right Along

Sami tent The Sami people live in Lapland, a region in far-northern Europe. In the spring, when nomadic Sami travel with their reindeer herds, they live in tents made of sticks covered with reindeer skins or canvas.

We usually think of a house as a building that stays in one place, but there are people all over the world who take their houses with them!

Nomads travel long distances in each season of the year, driving their cattle, sheep, or goats to places where there is grass. Tents made of woven goat hair, woven reeds and grasses, or animal skins are loaded onto horses, camels, or donkeys whenever the nomads move on. Each time the people stop, the tents are unloaded and set up.

Boats provide cozy homes for many people around the world. When children want to visit one another, the boats pull close and are tied together.

Yurt In Mongolia, goat herders live in round huts called *yurts*. The traditional yurt has a frame of wood over which is stretched a cover of felt made from pressed animal hair. A hole in the roof lets the smoke of the stove out. The only door faces south so the cold north wind cannot blow into the house.

Berber encampment, Tunisia The Berbers are a people who live throughout northwest Africa and the Sahara. Nomadic Berbers, who herd cattle, goats, and sheep, live in light, portable, goat-hair tents. These can be easily packed up and carried when the Berbers move to find new pastures.

Chinese junk In some Chinese cities, people live on houseboats called junks. In Hong Kong, there are whole neighborhoods where people live aboard houseboats.

Gypsy cart Gypsies are a nomadic people who have wandered throughout India, Asia, and Europe in their houses on wheels.

Houses that ride along roads on wheels are called mobile homes or trailers. Just like all houses, these may be big or small. In some countries, people put their houses on a cart pulled by a horse or mule. A house trailer might also ride along on separate wheels behind a car or truck. Some mobile homes look almost like buses. The driver sits near the front door and the rest of the house rolls along behind.

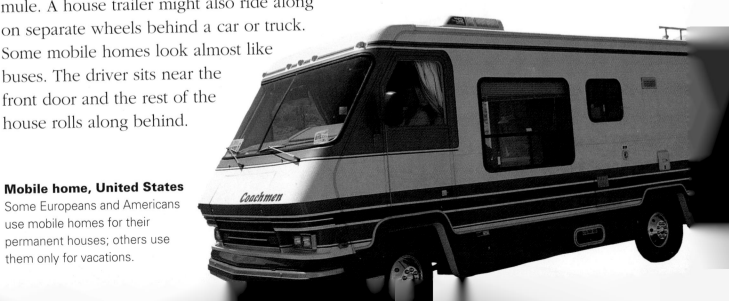

Mobile home, United States Some Europeans and Americans use mobile homes for their permanent houses; others use them only for vacations.

Houses That Work

Can you imagine a house that has a job? That's right, a house that works.

Lighthouses stand far out on windswept rocks or cliffs beside the ocean. These houses have a revolving light in a tower that warns the captains of ships at sea not to steer too close to the rocks. When it's foggy, the lighthouse sounds a fog horn, which makes deep honking noise that warns the ships to stay away from the rocks. The person who lives in the lighthouse is called the lighthouse keeper.

Another type of house that works is the fire lookout used by forest rangers. These houses are usually built on stilts and located high up on hills in the middle of forests. Forest rangers live in these houses for months at a time, but especially during dry months, when it is important to spot fires as soon as they start so that they can be put out quickly.

In some countries, truck drivers who spend weeks or months on the road make their trucks into houses. The truck is a working house because it carries freight and provides a place for the driver and assistant drivers

Pakistani Truck This truck driver uses his truck not only to haul freight, but also as a home while he is on the road for months. He has decorated his truck-house with bright colors and sayings so that it looks unique.

Lighthouse, United States The people who live in lighthouses make sure the lights and the horn are always working, and stay in contact with ships and with the shore to report on fog and storms.

to sleep and eat. Some of these trucks are decorated with with sayings and drawings so that they look special and feel like home.

Fishing boats are houses that work too. A fishing boat is a specially equipped house that has a place for nets on deck, cranes to life the nets, and storage holds for the fish that are caught. The boat also provides living space for the crew, who may be away from their homes on land for many months.

Canal barge, France Barges are flat-bottomed boats that carry freight to and from cities and towns in Europe along a network of canals. The owners of the barge make their home on the barge. When they take tourists for rides along the canals, it is just like visiting them in their homes.

Changing Houses

Over time, people everywhere have developed ways of building their houses to suit their everyday needs. Houses have changed as people have become better builders, as they have invented new systems and materials, and as they have earned more money.

Houses have also changed as people learn more about how to live in better harmony with their environment. In Pakistan, houses are cooled by special air scoops and fans rather than by electric air conditioning. In the Netherlands, some houses have solar panels on the roof to collect the heat from the sun to heat water for bathing. In Israel, special faucets and toilets help to conserve water in a desert environment.

Houses are also changing to accommodate people with physical disabilities. People who use wheelchairs, for example, can live in homes that have ramps instead of stairs, and kitchens that have lower counters, stoves, and sinks.

Not everything needs to be new or changing about houses.

Biosophere II Scientists lived in this specially constructed house in Arizona without ever going outside for two years! They studied how the occupants of a house can grow their own food, produce their own water, recycle materials they use, and continue to live together in harmony.

Genesis I Genesis I is a project to provide housing for the homeless in Los Angeles, California. These round, plastic homes were inexpensive to build because they are made of recycled materials.

Victorian house, United States
This beautiful old house, built in the 1800s, is being restored and preserved so that people can continue to live in it today.

House with solar panels Solar panels, which collect energy from the sun, can be a cost-saving way to heat the water people use inside their homes.

Older houses represent the history of people. As you have seen, houses can teach us a great deal about how people lived in the past as well as how they live in the present. From old houses we can learn what worked and what didn't in building and design. For this reason, in many parts of the world, people are learning about how best to preserve older houses.

No matter how houses change over time or how different they are around the world, each person makes their house a special place. After all, it takes the people in the house to make it a home.

Glossary

abundant more than enough; plentiful (p.6)

accommodate make suitable for (p.30)

ancestors relatives who lived in the past (p.20)

climate the average weather conditions of a region over a period of years (p.4)

communal having to do with or belonging to a group of people (p.19)

compound a fenced or walled yard with buildings inside (p.19)

corrugated having a ridged surface (p.11)

densely populated a lot of people living within a given area (p. 16)

distinguish to recognize one thing among others (p.24)

elaborate having much detail (p.24)

environment a person's natural surroundings (p.6)

fiberglass a flexible material made of glass spun into filaments (p.9)

framework the basic structure around which a thing is built (p.6)

generation a group of people who were born about the same time (p.23)

insulated surrounded with material that keeps heat or cold from leaking out or in (p.12)

intricate complicated (p.21)

lattice a framework made of interlaced strips of wood or metal (p.6)

manufactured made in a factory (p.8)

mythology a collection of legendary stories (p.21)

nomads people who move from place to place instead of settling in one place (p.26)

pitched sloped (p.14)

prehistoric occurring before the time when humans began recording history through writing (p.4)

recycle to use a material again (p.30)

sacred holy (p.20)

scarce hard to find; not plentiful (p.9)

siblings brothers and sisters (p.18)

social status the position of a person within his or her society (p.4)

sod the top layer of the earth, especially when covered with grass (p.7)

symbolize to stand for or represent something (p.21)

temperate not having extremes of hot and cold (p.9)

thatch a roof covering of reeds or straw (p.6)

traditional handed down from generation to generation (p.22)

tundra a treeless plain of northern arctic regions (p.8)

veranda a long, open, outdoor porch, usually roofed, along the outside of a building (p.15)

whitewashed whitened by being coated with a mixture of lime and water (p.13)

Index

About the Author

Sylvia White has a Ph.D. in urban planning from UCLA. She is Professor Emerita of California State Polytechnic University, Pomona. She has lived and taught in Africa and Costa Rica, and has traveled extensively.